P3

PURPOSE - PRIDE - PROGRESS

—

RAISE YOUR BAR

DR. ANTHONY J. PERKINS

authorHOUSE®

AuthorHouse™
1663 Liberty Drive
Bloomington, IN 47403
www.authorhouse.com
Phone: 1 (800) 839-8640

Published by AuthorHouse 07/16/2019

ISBN: 978-1-7283-1926-1 (sc)
ISBN: 978-1-7283-1935-3 (e)

There are three valuable questions you should ask yourself periodically:

What is my **purpose**?

Do I incorporate **pride** in all that I do?

Is **progress** my ultimate goal?

Prayer

God, please utilize this book to strengthen skills,
lift up people, and brighten journeys.
Help each reader to find their
purpose, take pride in every moment of life, and make
tremendous progress in all that comes before them.

CONTENTS

PART THREE

INTRODUCTION

What do you really need in life? Besides the obvious, food and water, you might consider achieving happiness, knowing your *purpose*, having positive relationships, taking *pride* in what you do, finding a soulmate, having peace in your life, and realizing *progress*. Let's focus on three replies—purpose, pride, and progress. There are three valuable questions you should ask yourself periodically:

What is my **purpose**?

Do I incorporate **pride** in all that I do?

Is **progress** my ultimate goal?

When there is a task to complete, an important life event, or a desire to increase your personal development, it is important to appreciate and incorporate into your life purpose, pride, and progress.

Notice how money is not mentioned above. Money is a temporary pleasure. Believe it or not, it is better to be rich with purpose, pride, and progress than to have all the money in the world. If you do not believe this, keep living.

How would you apply these three components to an aspect of your life? Let's use happiness as an example. Is your purpose to dole out happiness to a select few or to share it with the masses? How will you integrate pride while distributing happiness? Will it be a low-key endeavor or a loud and proud affair? What does progress in dispensing happiness look like? Is it measured in the amount of people touched by your happiness, or is it evident in a single smile? Asking questions then answering those questions by utilizing an action plan is an effective method to help you realize purpose, pride, and progress.

Approximately 50% of marriages end in a divorce, more than 70% of people don't feel satisfied with their careers, and a low percentage of people achieve success with their goals. Purpose, pride, and progress, when truly understood, can help people overcome these unfortunate trends. Let's dive below the surface and explore how purpose, pride, and progress can help you raise *your* bar in many aspects of life.

PART ONE

What is my purpose?

THINK

How different would your life be if you
followed your true purpose?
What sacrifices do you need to make
to achieve your purpose?

PURPOSE DEFINED

pur·pose
noun

Definition: The reason for which something
is done, created, or exists.
Example: The purpose of this book is to help
people reflect on and improve their lives.

Part one will invite you to find and utilize
your purpose to rise to a higher level.

Purpose is a calling. It is an instinct, an intuition, and a gut feeling that constantly stays with you. If you are open to receive it, you become more expanded; you become bigger and better because of it. Many people use their purpose to fight the good fight, finish the race, keep the faith, and do right with their time on Earth. Each of us has a purpose. Yes, we truly do. Are you utilizing your purpose to the maximum extent? Are you employing your purpose partially? Are you engaging your purpose in no way at all?

If your answer was *partially* or *in no way at all*, remember that time is precious and before you know it, it will be too late. Do not let a bad situation become a critical reminder for you to recognize your purpose. Engage now! Many people get caught up in excuses and thus fail to realize their purpose. They say: "After I get married, I will concentrate on my purpose." Or: "When my kids grow up, I will work on my purpose." Or even: "After I travel the world, I will focus on my purpose." The list of justifications goes on, but by the time these people have exhausted their excuses, they are too old and tired to accomplish anything. Figuratively speaking, their name is now placed on a box stored in a large warehouse with millions of other boxes that contain purposes that were never realized. This is the difference between people who make things happen and people who sit idly by as the world happens around them.

Do you know where the richest places are around the world? *Graveyards.* Why? Because, buried there are people who never started that business, never wrote that book, never sang that song, or never saw that innovation to fruition. These people were rich with purpose, but they never followed through.

As the saying goes, shoot for the stars because the bottom is overcrowded. From my many life experiences, this is a valid statement. You must use your purpose to make an impact. Be great with it. You are not reading this book by chance; this is another reminder to get going.

People always tell me they want to write a book. They end their sentences with *but* . . . followed by an excuse. As I once heard a pastor say during a church service, "You had better get that good china out and use it before the Lord comes." The same applies to your purpose: It's waiting for you to pull it out and share it with the world.

U se your purpose to conquer mountains. A "mountain" can be anything you want to accomplish. Is it your purpose to own a business, help a youngster, or teach college courses? Whatever your purpose, keep it in front of you by writing it down and posting it everywhere possible. Writing your purpose on paper will keep you focused on it, while also storing it in your subconscious for better retention.

When you conquer one mountain, seek a new challenge. Never stop at only one mountain. Your purpose has no expiration date. Would you help someone beat a drug addiction and then stop offering support? Would you reach a personal goal and then stop setting future goals? When you reach a new level in your marriage, do you stop trying? When you win, do you stop trying to succeed? **When you have achieved something great, keep going. Push yourself to do *BIGGER* things.**

Now is the time to seize the moment; you have shifted your confidence to a higher level, and you know you can accomplish much more. What makes you so sure? Your instinct is telling you to continue—don't ignore it. Do not waste this opportunity. Accomplishments do not come easy; however, you can conquer many mountains. Part of your purpose in life is continuous achievement.

By conquering mountains, you form a new mindset. Use this new mindset to teach others how to become focused and disciplined so that they might conquer their own mountains. Help others to achieve; achieving is about everyone enjoying success. Make it a best practice to share and help others. Assume everyone can be victorious.

ACTION PLAN

What mountain do you tackle first? You start by prioritizing. Ask yourself what is working in your life and consider where your focus should be. Begin with mountains that need immediate attention. For example, if your goal is to finish your education and start a business, conquer your education mountain first, because it is very difficult to complete an education and start a business at the same time. By finishing your education first, you will have the knowledge necessary to achieve the financial means required to start and lead your business. To conquer your mountains, you must prioritize.

LEAVING A LEGACY

Expect your legacy to touch millions of lives. I once heard the words, "Make a choice to sink or swim, float or flounder to transform from ordinary to briefly extraordinary." When examining your legacy, important questions to ask and answer are: What legacy will you leave through your purpose? What legacy will you leave now and later? Will your legacy contribute to the overall improvement of our world? If so, what does this improvement look like? Will your legacy be global, national, local, or all three? Answering these questions truthfully can lead to a fruitful legacy.

Now is the time to step up and be assertive in your life. Remember, nothing changes without movement. Be cautious to ensure your assertiveness is not negative, meaning cutthroat or used in a mean manner. Use your assertiveness as a tool to get things done. It is time to drop the rationalizing, jump in, and just do it.

Do not allow defeat or mediocrity to keep you from missing your legacy. Take pride and follow through. If you truly want to leave a legacy, understand you are doing the legacy work from your heart and care little about whether people realize the time and effort you put into the work. Be humble; the notoriety will come. There is no room for *kind of* or *sort of.* **Legacies command a confident emotional state that leads to positive actions and great results.** What is your legacy going to be?

ACTION PLAN

When you create your legacy, consider this advice:

- ✓ Take your time and think it through.
- ✓ Be very specific.
- ✓ Make your legacy an exciting journey with an impact.
- ✓ Believe anything can be accomplished if you are hungry enough.
- ✓ Identify support and training you might need.
- ✓ Keep your legacy in front of you by creating a vision board, rehearsing your legacy in your mind daily, and writing your legacy on sticky notes and placing them in key areas.
- ✓ Do not waver from your legacy. Fight for it.
- ✓ Have the courage to defeat the bad and ugly periods that could deter you from your legacy.

When it comes to your purpose, you cannot settle for "good enough." Do you want good relationships or great relationships? Do you want a good career or a great career? Do you want a good life or a great life? I am sure you answered *great* to all three questions, so why would you be fine with just a "good" purpose? Too many people are satisfied with good. *Don't be.* **Don't have a *just get by* attitude; always have a *this is my purpose* boldness.** Make your purpose a positive, noticeable endeavor.

What is the difference between a good purpose and a great purpose? Mother Theresa's purpose in life was to lead missionaries of charity around the world. She made a global impact. Her love and drive to help others was greatness at its pinnacle. She could have simply served in her village, which would have been nice and good. But not great.

Are you being patient and stretching yourself to be great? Or are you in a hurry and settling for good? Plenty of people are considered average—are you going to be one of them? If your answer is *no*, what are you going to be great at? How will you fulfill your purpose?

What separates good from great? Geno Auriemma, head women's basketball coach and 11-time national champion at the University of Connecticut states, "The difference between good and great basketball players is, good players get tired and great players do not. When good players get tired, great players kick their butts." In boxing, the difference between good and great boxers is, great boxers dig deep and find the will to finish the match strong. The difference between good and great people is effort. Great people understand they must sacrifice and go through many failures to be great.

ACTION PLAN

Jim Collins, author of *Good to Great*, states, "Level Five Leaders (great leaders) are humble and have a professional will to be great. If leaders want a great team, they must get the right people on the bus, get the wrong people off the bus, and move the right people in the right seats on the bus."

The difference between *ordinary* and *extraordinary* is the word *extra*. You must put in that extra effort to be great. The same principle applies to all areas of life. If you want to be a great husband or wife, put in the extra effort. If you want to be a great father or mother, put in the extra effort. If you want to be a great role model for children, put in the extra effort. Always choose great over good.

"Hello, operator, I would like to make a call to the world."

"Sure, what is the purpose of your call?"

"Well, I realize I am one runner in a relay race. I am one of many in an organization. I am one of several in a family. I am one of billions in the world. **My message to the world: When you are crafting your purpose, think multiple.**"

Is your purpose a gift just for you, or will you share it with others? Recently, I asked high school seniors to include third graders in their graduation ceremony. Here is how it would look: The school principal would lead the ceremony with various guest speakers stating words of encouragement throughout the program. At a key point in the ceremony, each senior would come to the podium, state their name, and list the college they would be attending or career they would be entering. Then, the senior would call up a third grader, state the youngster's name, and hand them an academic baton. Inside the baton would be a note from the senior expressing words of inspiration to graduate and make an impact in life. This would motivate the younger generation to graduate on time and would be seen as a passing-of-the-torch and giving-something-back gesture.

After much discussion about this recommendation, the seniors did not want to include this activity in their graduation ceremony. Instead, they decided to do it during a third-grade honor-roll assembly at the end of the school year. Perhaps one day I will convince the seniors to do this during an actual high school graduation. However, I do appreciate that they still wanted to participate in this endeavor.

ACTION PLAN

It is important that your purpose benefits you but also influences others. How can you use your purpose in a family setting? When your kids come to you and ask you to play with them, say "yes" no matter how tired you are. Why? You will never get that time back. Even if it is just for five minutes, do it. Instead of using those minutes to rest, use them to make a difference. Ask yourself: What is my purpose as a parent? Do not make this moment one to regret. When your kids get older and leave the home, if you did not play with them, you will wish you had those five minutes back. Use this example with all people. The most valuable gift you can give anyone is your time. How will your purpose shape the lives of others?

"Tear down this wall!" is a line from a speech given in West Berlin, in 1987, by former U.S. President Ronald Reagan. Reagan was calling for the General Secretary of the Communist Party of the Soviet Union, Mikhail Gorbachev, to open the border that had divided West and East Berlin since 1961. This notion can apply to your purpose. You can use your purpose to tear down walls in your personal and professional worlds. What are those walls you are facing? Is it an addiction? Is it a failed relationship? Is it a project you have been wanting to start for years?

Being conservative with your purpose is like becoming a leader and doing nothing with your influence. Adopt a courageous attitude with your purpose. You do not want to have remorse at the end of your days. Think of the brave people who have come before us and who have knocked down walls, great figures such as Abraham Lincoln, Jackie Robinson, Thomas Edison, and Albert Einstein.

Some people are caught up in a *This is the way it's always been* mentality. Be the one to educate them on how an open mind can advance people to make a situation better. When you enrich and shape others, you are helping them tear down walls. In the case of Berlin, tearing down the wall in 1989 led to many positive changes, such as reuniting families, resurrecting a shared culture, and integrating western ideas.

ACTION PLAN

What will be your wall to tear down? Consider joining an organization, association, or club that has a goal to overcome a challenge. There are many animal organizations working on stopping cruelty toward animals. There are organizations that feed the hungry. There are associations that fight cancer. There are clubs that clean up neighborhoods. Perhaps becoming a local advocate or politician can be your charge to tear down walls.

I t is important to frequently refresh your mind, body, and spirit. The daily minutiae can wear you down, causing you to stray from your purpose. Stay alert and be ready for this. Stress notoriously derails humans from their purpose. People will not always celebrate you while you work toward your purpose. Life can be complex because people can be complex. **Remember, people do not control your purpose. Only you govern your purpose**.

Make it a daily practice to rejuvenate. If you wait too long to recharge, negative thinking will start to recruit its buddies: stress, anger, depression, anxiety, and emotion. This event can harm the mind, body, and spirit. Emphasize your committed purpose. There are many people who lose sight of their purpose and never regain it. They believe they will return to it, someday, but then experience regrets later in life. A temporary setback is understandable; a permanent setback is inexcusable. Consistently refresh and make your purpose an exciting journey.

ACTION PLAN

Many trees shed their leaves during the fall only to grow new leaves each spring. When we first put on our clothes each day, notice how they are clean with no wrinkles, smelling good and looking sharp on us. Conversely, by the end of the day, our clothes are dirty with wrinkles. We then need to wash or dry clean (refresh) them to bring them back to their excellent state. These instances remind us to make *refreshing* a daily practice. It is important to establish routines to rejuvenate your mind, body, and spirit. Meditation, long walks, jogging, yoga, reading a great book, relaxing to your favorite music, spending time with a loved one, attending church, or reading a calming massage can reintroduce you to your purpose. Moving away from your purpose can happen. Expect it, but quickly transition back to your purpose by partaking in daily refreshing activities.

Incorporate leaving a deposit as part of your purpose. A deposit is anything positive that you say or do. **Make it a goal to leave a daily, weekly, monthly, or yearly deposit.** The more frequent the deposit, people will understand you are an influencer and game changer. This genuine action will send a message. People will appreciate that you are spreading positivity in the world.

With social media, the internet, television, and the speak-your-mind society hard at work polluting our world with lies, half-truths, or opinions, strive to be a person of excellence who is great in all aspects of life. Don't just reach for the stars, become a legend. People remember legends because they leave deposits in life. What deposits will you leave with young people, elders, or in your larger community?

Observe others and consider their deposits that inspired you. Was it great advice that helped you? Did they take you under their wing and teach you? Did they encourage you when you were down? The *deposit* concept can be utilized at any age and in all areas of life.

ACTION PLAN

If you have not started your deposit revolution, today is a great day to begin. Here are some examples of deposits: volunteering at a hospital, holding a door open for a stranger, giving a compliment, visiting a friend, buying a gift for a peer, sending a thank-you email to a colleague at work, calling a family member and wishing them well, and serving lunch at a homeless shelter.

Utilize your purpose to stand out, to separate yourself from the pack, and to aim high. Do not reserve any time for the people at the bottom who are hosting their own pity parties. Understand that life can be unfair at times; there will be difficult situations. Realize but don't accept the fact that people get jealous. Everyone can be successful, but only a small percentage of people go after victory. Why? Because the couch is more comfortable than success.

Think about this: If two people are taking the same journey across the desert and, halfway along, one person quits and returns to the starting point, both people have traveled the same distance. The difference is that one person believed in his or her purpose and the other person gave up on it. What are you going to do when life gets ugly? I encourage you to keep moving forward because the same-old, same-old is at the starting point.

Consider this poignant notion: *Everyone wants a rainbow, but few will persist through the storm and rain to see it.* It makes no sense to sit around and have a pity party, because after the pity party, the concern still exists. How many people do you know who have failed, chosen *not* to have a pity party, and then overcame their bad circumstances? The answer: very few. Support this trend and truth by remembering that every day is a new beginning. If you are having a bad day today, start over tomorrow. Stay committed and disciplined to your purpose. Give no energy to pity parties.

ACTION PLAN

When a pity party enters into your thinking, shift your mindset.

- ✓ Don't let your emotions control your motion. Step away, refocus, and then return.
- ✓ Pity parties take a lot of energy. Instead, use your energy to be amazing.
- ✓ Appreciate all the positive things in your life. You will discover there are more positives than negatives.
- ✓ Don't leave out God. He promises that no weapon formed against you shall prosper.
- ✓ Remember: Storms are temporary when you are dedicated to your purpose.

Let's review some key points in part one . . .

- ✓ When you have achieved something great, keep going. Push yourself to do *BIGGER* things.
- ✓ Legacies command a confident emotional state that leads to positive actions and great results.
- ✓ Don't have a *just get by* attitude; always have a *this is my purpose* boldness.
- ✓ My message to the world: "When you are crafting your purpose, think multiple."
- ✓ Being conservative with your purpose is like becoming a leader and doing nothing with your influence.
- ✓ Remember, people do not control your purpose. Only you govern your purpose.
- ✓ Make it a goal to leave a daily, weekly, monthly, or yearly deposit.
- ✓ Utilize your purpose to stand out, to separate yourself from the pack, and to aim high.

NOTES

What profound insights from this section will you immediately use to reach your purpose?

PART TWO

Do I incorporate pride in all that I do?

THINK

We know that when we take pride in things
we do, the results are plentiful.
So why don't we take pride in *all* that we do?

PRIDE DEFINED

pride
noun

Definition: A feeling, deep pleasure, or satisfaction derived
from one's achievements.
Example: I take great pride in dressing
professionally. He swallowed his
pride and asked for help.

Part two will review how to utilize pride
to make your life more rewarding.

WANTED: Pride.

Where has pride gone? Because people have turned life into a rat race, pride has taken a backseat in our values. Recently, at the grocery store, I approached the deli counter to purchase two salmon filets. But no associate was available to help me. I waited for about one minute and then a couple walked up and stood beside me. There were now three people waiting for service. About 15 seconds later, the deli employee arrived at the counter, and, as I was about the ask for the filets, the couple asked for help. They knew I was there first, but they took pride in helping themselves rather than waiting their turn.

As a society, we need to revisit pride and answer serious moral questions. For example, has the convenience of technology hurt pride? We seem to take more pride in technology than we do in people. Do *you* take pride in others? There are many people who participate in comparing rather than celebrating others. If someone is doing better than you, learn from them and celebrate their success. Why do some individuals still have a problem with people of color? We are all created equal and we should respect all cultures.

Why is poor leadership accepted at the global, national, and state levels? As a leader, you are a role model and your body of work should positively impact others. I encourage everyone to reexamine how they take pride in self, family, faith, property, community, and mankind. One lyric in the song "We Are the World" says: *We are the world, we are the children. We are the ones who make a brighter day, so let's start giving.* If we are to achieve this result, we must integrate pride in all areas of our lives.

Pride can be good or bad depending on how we approach it. If we have a great work ethic, if we are an awesome parent, if we help others, or if our daily practice is simply being a person with excellent character, we can proudly state that we are a person with great pride. Not taking responsibility, being loud and too boastful about your deeds, and believing the world owes you everything is considered bad pride.

The Bible's Book of Proverbs reminds us that having too much pride will cause us to make mistakes, leading to setbacks or failure. In other words, pride can come before a fall. How do you handle pride? Do you have an attitude of gratitude for your successes, no matter how big or small, or do you engage in an over-the-top celebration—as if you could now walk on water because of what you have accomplished? Now is the time to be honest. Remember that the goal is to reflect and improve. There is a reason why you are reading this section. If your answer is the latter, thinking you walk on water because of your successes, I recommend you take time to think, put yourself in other people's shoes, and then adopt a more humble approach.

When pride is applied in a bad manner, the paths that you take on your journey will be filled with delays or obstructions. People stop wanting to be around you, they stop liking you, and they start talking about you. Our successes come from a higher power. Be grateful for your opportunities, endeavors, and talents; there is no need to be flashy with the positive impact you are making in life. People will notice your positive ambition, energy, and grit. People with great pride don't care whether others know of their attainments. This may come across as common sense, but remember: Common sense is not always common practice.

ACTION PLAN

People with great pride hold these attributes:

- ✓ They possess a positive personality. They are *I can, I will* people.
- ✓ They always have good intentions.
- ✓ After an achievement, they celebrate in a humble manner.
- ✓ They take pride in making other people shine.
- ✓ They do more than what is expected.
- ✓ They challenge themselves to always bear fruit.
- ✓ They leave a situation in better shape than it was when they found it.
- ✓ They stand out.

A nalyze your temptations and make a commitment to conquer them. Temptations are typically bad habits. Temptations will come, and they are different for every person. A temptation can be spending too much money, being impatient, speaking your mind, using drugs, drinking too much alcohol, smoking, or overeating.

Some people think temptations are okay if enjoyed in small doses, but temptations deter us from doing the right thing. Here is something to think about: Many people have died after experimenting with only small amounts of drugs. Also, some people are tempted to drink too much alcohol on a consistent basis due to depression, stress, or other factors. Statistics state that 70% of alcoholics do not think they have a drinking problem. Drinking alcohol may temporarily remove the negative feelings a person has, but once the alcohol effect diminishes, the individual's underlying problems still exist. You can reduce temptation by:

- ✓ Surrounding yourself with positive people. Positive people tend to be upbeat, and they discipline themselves to eliminate temptations from their thinking.
- ✓ Seeking out successful people to be your mentors. Mentors can guide you to stay on course.
- ✓ Removing yourself from people and locations that ignite your temptations. If you are trying to stop being an angry person, discontinue associating with other angry people. If certain locations cause you to

be angry, stop going to those locations. Here, the saying *Out of sight, out of mind* applies.

The temptation to smoke has increased thanks to the emergence and marketing of new vaping products. Will people allow small smoking devices to dictate their lives? Will they let a small thing stop them from going a long way? **You cannot conquer what you will not confront.** Be honest about your temptations. Understand you become a slave to what controls you.

ACTION PLAN

What is a key factor to take control of your temptations? The answer is discipline. Discipline is not only what you do, it is what you *do not* do. To eliminate a temptation from your life, take baby steps. Why? Our mind and body need time to accept and then adjust to the fact that the temptation will no longer be a part of our being. When doctors treat patients who are addicted to drugs such as crack cocaine and methamphetamine, they slowly wean individuals off these drugs, decreasing the dosage rather than immediately stopping the intake. Addicts are likely to die if their minds and bodies are not allowed to accept and then adjust to the new reality.

It is essential to stay disciplined during the weaning process. Once a drug addict has recovered from taking drugs, many recovered addicts set small day-to-day goals to resist the urge of future drug temptations. One daily goal could be to stay away from drug-infested neighborhoods, as well as people who are using drugs. Such precautions could apply to all temptations. What are the temptations that you need to examine and overcome? Insert your discipline to take great pride in beating your temptations.

C onsider making a promise to take pride in your body. **The only time we have is the time in which we are living: the here and now.** We have been given a beautiful instrument called the body. We are given one lifetime to positively condition our bodies, physically and mentally. Recently, at a function, I met a married couple who were most likely in their late fifties but who had the bodies of 38-year-olds. They told me that they made a promise to each other to keep their bodies in the best shape possible so they could live a long life together. I could see they were sticking to that agreement, because their skin looked healthy and their bodies were toned. Many of us have witnessed mothers who have had multiple babies but who have returned their bodies to their pre-baby state by staying active and watching their diets. In both cases, the pride to take care of the body is to be commended. These are uncommon people.

I say these next words respectfully: Why do people let their bodies go after getting married? Why do they continue to overeat and then wonder why they are obese? The health statistics suggest that many people are unhealthy due to bad diets and a lack of exercise. In today's world, because of social media, radio, and television, everyone understands what a healthy lifestyle involves; still, many people ignore the research. I have even met doctors who know smoking is bad for the body, and yet they continue to smoke.

About one year ago I was 23 pounds heavier. I was that slender guy with a belly, and I started wearing my casual shirts untucked to hide it. When I went to work, I would wear vests to create the illusion that I was slimmer. I finally said to myself, "I'm not going out like this." Just because I am getting old does not mean I am going to give myself permission to become fat and ugly.

I thought I had been eating a healthy diet but then realized I had not. This was when I said to myself, "Anthony, what are you going to do?" After reviewing my diet and exercise routine, I concluded that I was failing myself. I had significantly reduced my exercise routine, dropping to only once a week. There were many weeks that I did not exercise at all. I realized that I was sitting many hours at work as well as during the hour and 20 minutes I spent commuting to and from work. My diet consisted of many carbohydrates (e.g., pasta, rice, bread, and yogurt), sweets, and very few if any vegetables, nuts, plants, and fruits. Contrary to popular belief, yogurt is not good for you. Just check the label. They don't tell you that in the commercials.

I decided to start a healthy diet by cutting carbohydrates by 80%, while also reducing sweets by 80%, decreasing my alcohol intake by 80%, and becoming more physically active during the week. Additionally, I added fish to my diet. During the work week, I pack my lunch bucket with fruits, nuts, water bottles, and salads (no dressing). Sweets are no longer welcome in my office. I walk six or nine miles every weekend and work out twice a week.

Within two weeks of staying disciplined to my new routine, I lost seven pounds. I then went on a 10-day weight-loss cleanse, which taught me much more about the body, mind, and dieting. I lost another 11 pounds from the cleanse. There were times when my mind and body acted like I was starving, but I stayed the course with my routine and the cravings went away. You are retraining your mind and body when you improve your diet and physical fitness routine. Never waver from the plan, and you will see results. This is where many people give up—not realizing they were so close to breaking their unhealthy behaviors.

Overall, I am very happy to report that I lost 23 pounds during this transition. Even better, I maintain this routine. I have my cheat days but then return to my diet. My blood pressure is great, along with my cholesterol level. I feel light, energetic, and the belly is gone. There are times in life when you think you are doing well but are actually living a lie. The key is to be honest with yourself and fix the problem. This experience was a great lesson for me.

ACTION PLAN

There are five Blue Zone regions in the world where people live much longer than average. Many people in these Blue Zones live beyond 100 years of age. The people inhabiting Blues Zones share common lifestyle characteristics that contribute to their longevity. Blue Zone people take pride in:

- ✓ Eating a plant-based diet (semi-vegetarianism).
- ✓ Having a life purpose.
- ✓ Having a stress-reduction plan.
- ✓ Constant moderate physical activity.
- ✓ Moderate caloric intake.
- ✓ Moderate alcohol intake, if any.
- ✓ Not smoking.
- ✓ Engaging in spirituality or religion.
- ✓ Engaging in family life.
- ✓ Engaging in a social life.

I recommend starting with a few of these Blue Zone habits and adding more Blue Zone characteristics in time. You will become a healthier and more vibrant person. What will be your promise that you will take pride in?

EVERYTHING STARTS IN YOUR THINKING

A young man approached his pastor and informed him that he was selling drugs to make money. The young man told the pastor he knew it was wrong and dangerous, but that other members of his family were also selling drugs. He felt he had no chance of beating the odds to become successful because his home life was so dysfunctional. The pastor said,

> Son, you are fooling yourself and you're better than this. When you sell drugs, you must market the product. That's marketing. You need to get the word out. That's advertising. You must take care of your clients. That's customer service. You need to know when to sell and when not to sell. That's a management decision. Son, if you can sell drugs, you can sell stocks and bonds, medical equipment, electronics, or furniture.

The point is, everything starts in your thinking. When you are making decisions, choices, or judgments, take pride in reaching your goal or destination the right way. **There is a saying: You can do things right or you can do the right thing.** In the case of the young man mentioned above, did his environment lead him to think peddling drugs was the only way to make money? Could he have transcended his circumstances and come up with positive and legal alternatives for making money?

It is easy to think clearly and take pride when there is no pressure and nothing is on the line. However, how do you handle pride when there is stress to produce results at work, when your child is off course, when you have a medical concern, when a loved one dies, or when finances are tight and you need to make money quickly? Make the decision to choose pride over stress. A stressful decision can lead to many bad consequences. You will go through tough times in life. No one is exempt from the bad and ugly that life dishes out. Believe everything is lined up for you and go for it. Challenge yourself to step up to new levels. Be a person who lifts people, heals people, saves people, and feeds people. Leave your mark. **P**eople **R**espond to **I**nfluence, **D**rive, and **E**nergy-PRIDE.

ACTION PLAN

Let's use the example of taking pride in selecting your career. Understand that there is a difference between a job and a career. A job is temporary. Teenagers and college students have jobs. Some adults take on a job in addition to their careers in order to pay their bills. A career is a long-term position that people strive to achieve.

When selecting a career, answer these questions honestly:

- ✓ What are you great at?
- ✓ What do you love doing?
- ✓ What is a skill you have always wanted to pursue?
- ✓ What have past bosses complimented you on?

Answering these questions will give you a great start in determining a career path. There will be many obstacles in attaining your career choice, but if you believe you can overcome, you will. Do not be in a hurry; good things come to those who are patient. Never let someone else keep you from your career. *You* control your destiny.

Take pride in pushing yourself to grow and increasing your performance to brilliance. Keep building your capacity. Strive to get better in areas that need improvement. Taking the first step can be scary, but dive in. You will discover that it gets easier as you move closer to your goal. If you have an urge that has been eating away at you, this is your sign to go for it. Shift your motivation and confidence into a higher gear and rise up. You know it is hard work, but remember that hard work reaps rewards.

What area are you trying to grow? Is it in your marriage, your learning, your parenting, your fitness, your relationships, your faith, or your financial wellness? When you determine your *what*, you will realize you need to take a leap of faith. **When you put action behind your thinking, you will feel a burden lifted from your mind.** You will have a stronger sense of self and will feel a sense of accomplishment.

No matter your age, you can always grow in some areas. Yes, the wiser you become, the more you have to offer; but you also have much still to learn. Ask yourself if you are perfect. The answer will always be *no*. This means you have areas in life to grow.

People move through life in different ways. Some choose a path of least resistance (no growth); others take a path of exploring, discovering, and realizing (growth). It is easy to not grow. Just sit around and do a bunch of nothing.

ACTION PLAN

How do you know when you are growing as a person?

- ✓ When others can't do something, you can.
- ✓ You have a sense of decency, a sense of optimism.
- ✓ You use an opportunity to become better.
- ✓ You understand that once you have tasted great, *good* does not work for you anymore.
- ✓ You recognize that you went down so you could come up. You cried so you could rejoice. You did without so you could overcome.-Bishop T.D. Jakes

DON'T GO WITH THE FLOW

Take pride in not going with the flow. You do not have to go with popular thinking. Be unusual, be different. However, do things in a classy manner. There is no need to be rude, mean, or difficult. It is easy to go with the flow but expect the same results. Be able to explain your position with facts, data, or research. Offer a description of how the unfamiliar can catapult or quantum leap people, organizations, or the situation. **Be intelligent and sharp when standing out. If you are ignorant, people will treat you that way.** This approach may decrease how people will judge your stance. A separation-from-the pack mentality could cause people to unfairly conclude you are defiant, difficult, or a diva.

Think of a brook and its flowing water. Consider the water as the status quo or people being comfortable—that is, not wanting to evolve. Now imagine inserting your finger in the flowing brook and moving it against the natural flow of the water. You will create waves and feel resistance. This happens when you go against the flow, and it is where innovation, creativity, leadership, being a pioneer, heroism, and change can emerge. I want to emphasize, however: Go against the flow but do so in a positive manner.

ACTION PLAN

When you go against the flow, understand it will take all of your talents. You cannot do this halfway or half-heartedly. Appreciate these opportunities because they are irregular. Utilize your wisdom. Incorporate all of your knowledge, skills, and experience. Illustrate that your ideas are effective and will cause movement. Ensure your strategy is well-conceived, realistic, and tailored to the situation, while also including an influential component. If you can change the emotional state of individuals, the likelihood of changing their minds is high. Be genuine when pulling at their heartstrings. Trust that you can defy the odds when going against the flow.

W hy do people talk about winning? Winning seasons, winning opportunities—they do it because so much of life is about winning. We must win the object of our romantic interest, we must win at sports, we must win in our careers, or we must have a winning personality. To win, we convince ourselves that the setting must be right, the people in our lives must be right, and the timing must be right. If only it could be the way we dreamed it up.

Take pride in winning and losing. Another word for losing is *learning*. Jack Nicklaus, also known as the Golden Bear, is considered the greatest golfer ever due to his impressive record of winning 18 major golf championships. As of 2019, Tiger Woods has won 15 major golf championships. I once heard Jack Nicklaus state in an interview, "If you place second in a golf competition, be a classy runner-up. Shake hands, congratulate, take pride in your effort and the gentlemen that was victorious over you." These words are insightful. Ask yourself: Do you practice these characteristics when you lose (learn)? It is okay to lose as long as you have put in your best possible effort. Losing cultivates a person. If you were to win at everything, you would no longer try. Losses challenge us to analyze and ask ourselves many questions, such as: Was there a key factor that caused me to lose? Or: How could I have done things differently?

ACTION PLAN

How can you become a better winner and learner? Here is some guidance:

- ✓ Study thought leaders, influencers, and game changers. How do *they* handle being a winner and learner?
- ✓ Challenge yourself to transform any trouble into triumph.
- ✓ Have an attitude that you are not going to be at the same place next year.
- ✓ Challenge your mind to be clearer, your sense of purpose to be sharper, and your aptitude to be deeper.
- ✓ Don't settle, advance.

D ive into your commitments. Jump hurdles to keep them. Take pride in them.

What is a commitment? A commitment is being dedicated to a cause or activity. Some examples of commitments are finishing a project, spending time with your family, personal development, obtaining a degree, or teaching others. People commit to things that are important to them. I have one friend who is committed to family time, another who is committed to friend time, and another who is committed to "me" time.

Will you be able to keep 100% of your commitments? No, of course not. But the goal is to keep most of them. In life, you can choose to take pride in commitments or you can be cavalier. Which person are you going to be?

The definition of *conformity* is acting like everyone else, and its opposite could be courage. Conformism could involve struggling and depending on others for life's necessities. You could ask many people why they go to work and some would answer *I do because everyone else does*. This is conformity.

There was a case study conducted by Dr. Albert Schweitzer in which he took one hundred 25-year-olds and tracked their lives to age 65. These people were all eager and ready for success in life. One of their many goals was to become rich. Dr. Schweitzer's case study focused solely on whether these 25-year-olds became rich by age 65, and he found that one was rich, four were financially independent, and the rest were either still working or broke. This case study tells us that 5% (5 out of 100 people) achieved financial success. They overcame failures and persevered.

The remaining 95% hit a failure point and then conformed to one of the biggest norms in society: They gave up, perhaps thinking to themselves, *Well, at least I tried.* Don't settle for this, for average; pick yourself up and keep trying. This is what separates the "Make it happen" people from the people who wonder, *What happened?*

The progressive realization of a worthy idea is one definition of success; a person working toward a predetermined goal is another. **Successful people have goals and work toward achieving them. If they can't find success, they make it.** Successful people take pride in succeeding. Successful people understand they achieve nothing without paying a price. If you want to be a doctor, there will be many years of difficult study. Your peers and friends will complete their schooling, purchase homes, and start families before you. However, by staying the course with your medical education, you will be able to buy a bigger home and have a prettier wife or more handsome husband than your peers and friends. You may go without gratification for a longer time, but the end result will be bigger and better.

ACTION PLAN

How do you make a commitment?

- ✓ Don't be vague. Be exact—know what you need to commit to. Zero in on it, and be specific. For example, if you want to be happy, ask and answer these questions: Happy at what? When? Where? Why? How?
- ✓ Make your commitment a priority.
- ✓ Take steps to achieve your commitment if necessary. If your goal is to save 15% of your annual income, start by saving 5% in year one, 10% in year two, and 15% by year three.
- ✓ Have mentors who will hold you accountable to your commitments.
- ✓ Have a Plan B if your commitment does not work out. This is where some people give up.

How do you avoid conformity?

- ✓ Go out on a limb; this is where the fruit grows.
- ✓ Take risks.
- ✓ Get out of your comfort zone.
- ✓ Challenge yourself. You have so much in you.
- ✓ Don't follow the crowd. Make your own path.

What are traits of successful people?

- ✓ They become what they think about.
- ✓ When they earn something, they value it.
- ✓ They rise above narrow-minded people and petty prejudices.
- ✓ They use positive thinking to overcome negative thoughts.

Let's review some key points in part two:

- ✓ The Bible's Book of Proverbs reminds us that having too much pride will cause us to make mistakes, leading to setbacks or failure.
- ✓ You cannot conquer what you will not confront.
- ✓ The only time we have is the time in which we are living: the here and now.
- ✓ There is a saying: You can do things right or you can do the right thing.
- ✓ When you put action behind your thinking, you will feel a burden lifted from your mind.
- ✓ Be intelligent and sharp when standing out. If you are ignorant, people will treat you that way.
- ✓ Take pride in winning and losing. Another word for losing is *learning*.
- ✓ Successful people have goals and work toward achieving them. If they can't find success, they make it.

NOTES

Pride can be good or bad. What did you learn in this section that you will utilize immediately to practice pride effectively?

PART THREE

Is progress my ultimate goal?

THINK

How would you feel if you were making
progress in all areas of your life?
What would progress look like in all areas of your life?

PROGRESS DEFINED

prog·ress
noun

Definition: The forward or onward
movement toward a destination.
Example: One rejection did not stop
my progress toward my goal.

Now that you have learned about some critical
components of purpose and the importance of pride, let's
conclude with the significance of making progress in life.
Utilizing your purpose and taking pride in it will give
you forward movement, progress, in all facets of life.

Purpose, pride, and progress are three important fundamentals to continuously work on in life. Building your capacity daily in these areas will make you a better person, professionally and personally. Push yourself to be exceptional. Many people wish to remain ordinary; pass them by. Most will point their finger at something and say, "This is a problem," but only a few will fix the problem. Problem-solvers start by exhausting all ideas and possibilities and having more energy than the problem. Be *THAT* person. There will be wild highs and wild lows in your life, and they could come on the same day. How you react to these highs and lows is important. If you're at rock bottom, the only direction to go is up.

There is light and dark in all of us. Concentrate on being the light. Always keep one eye on the present and one eye on the future. Remember, formative experiences teach people to adjust and stir up greatness. Accept that having different perspectives in life is necessary. Diversity of perspectives moves the world forward.

Be careful with your judgments. How many times have you judged someone or something, only to be wrong? Raise your hand, because all of us are guilty of this. If you want to stop having regrets, then conquer your fear. We only get one journey in life, so make it a remarkable ride. It is time to be assertive in capturing the life you desire. It is time to raise *your* bar.

If you want to reach your goals, dreams, and destinations, you must be hungry. A hungry attitude means investing, seeking, searching, observing, learning, sacrificing, recovering from failure, and being unstoppable, no matter what. "Hungry" involves providing more service than you get paid for. You cannot have an attitude of getting paid more for doing more. That is selfish thinking. Hungry also entails dressing and living the role that you want to become.

Life is going to happen to you whether you want it to or not. There will always be the good, the bad, and the ugly. To reduce the bad and the ugly, be prepared. When life knocks you down, have comeback power. Be hungry to overcome challenges, barriers, and limitations. When things go wrong, don't go with them. Nobody can live your dream but you!

Surround yourself with OHP (Only Hungry People). Sometimes we lose our hunger. When you build relationships with only hungry people, there will always be someone in that circle to pick you up and restart your engine. Make it a habit to associate with only hungry people. There is a concept called *the law of the group* that states that when you hang around like-minded people, you act like them. For example, negative people tend to hang around other negative people. This concept applies to hungry people, too. Hanging around hungry people keeps you hungry.

ACTION PLAN

Give yourself permission to be and stay hungry by:

- Challenging yourself.
- Staying disciplined. Discipline is what you do and don't do.
- Learning daily.
- Living full, dying empty.
- Contributing to other people's lives.
- Doing right. In the words of Dr. Martin Luther King, "The time is always right to do right."
- Believing you can do more.

FLESH
VERSUS SPIRIT

Listening to your spirit can help you make progress in life. It is the common sense instinct that is guiding you in the right direction. Your spirit will tell you to be disciplined and to not spend money at this point. It will direct you to wait until the proper time. Your flesh will tell your mind to spend money, insisting that you deserve to do so. If you don't have the money now, just charge the purchase on your credit card and pay later. This is okay. Now is your time. You can always catch up later. Don't you want to have what others have right now? Your flesh pumps up your ego and does not remind you to stay within your budget. Do you want to be a person who only works to pay bills or a person who is wise with his or her money, a person with options?

If you truly want to make progress with your finances in life, you must understand financial wellness. Spending, spending, and more spending is not the answer. Hill Harper states, "You can't be free if the cost of being you is too high." The trap many people fall into when spending the little or huge sums of money they have is that they feel they deserve to spend. They justify their overspending with emotions. The flesh will insist that you deserve it, and it might continue with this fiction even after you run out of money. Money is like power: the more you have, the more options you have. The important thing is to be wise with it and to listen to your spirit.

ACTION PLAN

The concept of flesh versus spirit can apply to all areas of your life. Our spirit is trying to keep us from debt, bad decisions, and danger. The problem is that humans are very emotional and can often become a victim of their emotions. How do you know when your spirit is talking to you? You will know when your instinct (that inner voice) is trying to keep you within your boundaries, disciplined, and on track toward your goals. Your progress depends on your spirit. It is critical to listen to it and follow it.

You miss 100% of the shots you don't take, so take the shot. Too often we chicken out and miss our opportunity. How many more regrets are you going to add to your "I wish I had" list? Progress requires taking risks and getting out of your comfort zone. **Everyone who has done anything great has completed the accomplishment with fear.** How many times have you hesitated to do something, only to finish it later and say, "Wow, that was easier than I thought?" Take the shot.

We have all watched movies, documentaries, and TV shows that featured someone overcoming a tough situation. I tell students, "If I can write books, you can write better books. You just need to put in the time and effort." Fear of the unknown keeps humans from advancing. We should comprehend two ideas in our daily lives. The first is that very little in our lives is unknown; the second is that there will always be some unknowns in our daily lives. When these unknowns transpire, we analyze and conquer them, as we have in the past. We learn from these experiences and take on the attitude that it's just another unknown—and that is okay. We know people are imperfect, information can be misleading, and resources may not always be available. But we adapt, overcome, and improvise in order to make progress. Take the shot.

Talk over the negative thoughts in your head and disregard the negative people who do not believe in you. There will always be haters; some will be your friends and family members. Instead of celebrating you, they compare you to themselves. If you are advancing and they are not, their insecurities could cause them to dislike you. Let them worry about their self-doubt. When it comes to you, take the shot.

ACTION PLAN

Think of a boxing match where you are one of the fighters. You are getting ready in the locker room, knowing you will have to take that long walk through the crowd to the ring. Once you are ready, you start the walk and notice that everyone is booing you. People in the crowd are yelling things like, "You are going to lose!" and "You have no chance!" Once you arrive at the ring, settle in at your corner, and look across at your opponent, you notice something familiar about them: It's *you*! To reach your goals, dreams, and aspirations, you are fighting *you*. Your boss is not the enemy, your neighbor is not holding you back, and "The Man" is not oppressing you. The only one holding you back from progress is you. Take the shot.

NOTHING CHANGES UNTIL SOMETHING MOVES

M oving forward is easy when you know what direction to go. If you are down, choose to be up. Remember, no one controls your destiny but you. If you are traveling on a dangerous street, find another option. In other words, change your world. Easy choices lead to a hard life; hard choices lead to an easy life. Now that you know your direction, make progress by moving forward. Be strategic with your movements; understand a true winner seeks movement. **There are many actors, athletes, and everyday people who are always looking to not just reach their goals but crush them.** This growth mindset is necessary for progress in life.

Always believe you are not done yet. Can you invest more time and energy in your family, marriage, and career? If you do 20 push-ups today, believe that you can do 25 of them tomorrow. Never accept that doors are locked. Doors are opportunities, so open as many of them as there are prospects waiting for you. If a door closes on you, open another. Celebrate the good, discard the bad, and improve the ugly. Understand there will be people who do not agree with your moves. Ignore them. These people have a fixed mindset and will always lack progress in their lives.

ACTION PLAN

Change with movement results in progress. If you seek progress in life, consider these recommendations:

- ✓ Include faith in your life.
- ✓ Make family your top priority.
- ✓ Understand that living a "free life" is not worrying about money and death.
- ✓ Recognize that true happiness is achieved through positive relationships.

There is no finish line in life. Life is not like a video game where you reach the end and it says GAME OVER. When you finish something in life, it's time to move on to the next thing. However, do not be in a hurry to get to that next thing. Take pleasure in the steps that help you complete your journey. When your child asks you to go to his or her band concert next week, attend. Don't offer an excuse. This is time you will never get back, so make it count. **Learning to appreciate your journey is progress. It builds your character.**

We get so focused on accomplishing our goals that, when we finally reach them, sometimes we forget to take time to appreciate the hard work, beauty, and lessons learned along the way. Be careful of being in a hurry. Slow down and cherish your journey. You don't have to spend thousands of dollars to travel thousands of miles to enjoy life. Life is all around you. Stop, look, and listen. Spend time with your family, watch a sunset, tell loved ones how important they are to you, go to a movie, visit a museum, or meet an old friend at a coffee shop.

Youngsters, enjoy your elders. Once they are gone, their knowledge will go with them. Absorb as much from them as possible. Understand their trials and misfortunes so that you can avoid the same missteps. Shape your attitude, character, and integrity by learning about their successes.

Adults, your words are powerful. What can you say to encourage young people to push through a challenge? What words can you plant in a child's mind that will grow later in life to make them successful? How can you create an opportunity for someone?

ACTION PLAN

Here are some suggestions to help you appreciate your journey and make progress:

- ✓ Give back.
- ✓ Hang out with only high quality people.
- ✓ Read, read, read. This will increase your knowledge.
- ✓ Manage your time effectively.
- ✓ Take courses.
- ✓ Learn new skills.
- ✓ Take care of your body.
- ✓ Expand your network.
- ✓ Go for walks.
- ✓ Lend and do not borrow.
- ✓ Save and invest money.
- ✓ Stop procrastinating.

THE FIRST STEP

We have the power to make the world we envision but only if we have the courage to take the first **step**. If you want to make progress in life, take the first step. There are many people who don't realize how close they were to victory because they never took that first step. Did you know that when a rocket is launched it expends 50% of its total fuel? When a jet plane takes off, it uses 25% of its total fuel. The same concept applies to humans: When we take our first steps, we use a lot of energy because of our fears and doubts. My advice is to jump in—just do it! If things go wrong at first, don't go with them. Refuse to fail. No one can live your dream but you.

Take the first step to learning something new, to getting that guy or girl you desire, to purchasing that car you want, to earning that degree you need, to being a great father or mother to your kids, or to beating that drug addiction. As the expression goes, *90% of life is how you respond and 10% is what happens to you.* If you want to live a large life, you need to be a now person. Now, is the time to take that first step. You can do it.

ACTION PLAN

Imagine a path in front of you. Keep this path in the forefront of your mind whenever you are taking your first steps. Be creative with your imaginary path; it can be straight, curvy, zigzag, or whatever you choose. At the end of the path is your desire, goal, or achievement. Visualize walking down the path. Truly feel that focus. Remove the nonsense in your mind that is trying to distract you. Choose to stay the course and keep moving forward. Take on an attitude of "slaying the dragon" as you walk down your path. Remember, no one can take you there but you. Go beyond to reach your destination.

The world is full of concerns. We have the wage gap, the opportunity gap, the achievement gap, and the family gap to name a few. The conveniences of the world have made some people lose their connections to and as human beings. If we were all able to work from home, which some people do, we might never need to leave the house. Why? We can do almost everything online, including banking, paying bills, purchasing tickets, buying clothes, ordering food, setting up dry-cleaning services, arranging appointments for house cleaning, car, pet, and landscaping services, and visiting a doctor. We can even find our spouse online.

Some of these conveniences are good for us, but too much convenience can be bad for us. It can make us lazy, which actually hinders our progression. Because we can order other people to accomplish our goals for us on the internet, we lose our critical thinking skills and drive.

I love dark chocolate almonds. It is my favorite cheat food. However, after about ten of these almonds, I start to dislike the taste and my desire to eat more almonds fades. The same notion can apply to conveniences.

When are we going to start being humans again? How about if we start by getting back to looking each other in the eyes and having those face-to-face conversations? Let's bring back that old idea of the family eating dinner together at the dining table with the television off. What if we help each other out before an actual emergency happens? **Shifting our focus to family, curing deadly diseases, investing in education, and being great role models can be a start.**

ACTION PLAN

In the television series *Star Trek: The Next Generation* the goal of humanity is personal development not the pursuit of wealth. In *Star Trek* everything is given to you. If you want a cup of tea, go to the simulator and ask for it. This gives humans the time to grow intellectually. In the movie *Ready Player One* the objective was to win control of the Oasis, a virtual universe. The team that achieved this feat in the film decided to shut down the Oasis twice during the week so people could focus on family time and self-improvement.

I vote that we immediately turn off cell phone, television, and internet services every Sunday and Monday. Can we go back to roasting marshmallows over a camp fire in our backyards, loving one another, and appreciating the company of a friend or family member? Let's fly a kite, go fishing, and visit our grandparents before they transition. This is real progress. The new-school generation could learn many things from their older-school counterparts. I think I will use this as a platform when I run for president in 2028.

—

Another ingredient to making progress in your life is understanding there will be many times that pain will affect you. Pain comes in many forms, and it will change you. Pain can be related to your health. It can be a relationship pain, where someone walked out on you, or you can have a career pain, meaning you were passed over for a promotion. **Pain improves your character; it prepares you, increases you, and develops you.**

In the movie *Rocky III* Clubber Lang took on Rocky and predicted "PAIN" for Rocky during the boxing match. That is why Clubber lost the match. Every struggle with pain makes you better. You can get better from it or remain bitter from it. You can go through it or grow through it. When that next challenge with pain occurs, how are you going to handle it? Will you take the first step and approach pain differently? Will you adopt a positive attitude and overcome pain by rising like the sun every day?

ACTION PLAN

When you are dealing with a painful situation, thinking positive thoughts can help decrease the pain. Repeating positive affirmations can help you change your emotional state. Here are some affirmations to repeat in your thinking:

- ✓ I can overcome.
- ✓ I can do this.
- ✓ I can achieve.
- ✓ I will rebuild to become bigger, better, faster, and stronger.
- ✓ I will rebound.
- ✓ I will work hard to improve.
- ✓ I am better than this.
- ✓ I am smart.
- ✓ I am prepared.
- ✓ I am a good person.
- ✓ I am confident.
- ✓ I am special.
- ✓ I am important.
- ✓ I got this!

There is a concept called *pay it forward* that asks people to repay a good deed to someone other than the original benefactor. Close your eyes and think about a special person who has helped you, someone who made an impact in your life. It could be a person who taught you to tie your shoes as a kid. It could be a person who gave you encouragement before a job interview. Perhaps it was a person who set you up with an unexpected opportunity that you really needed. This person might still be a big part of your life or might have been in your life for only a moment.

It is now your turn to "pay it forward." If you want to improve your character, start by giving back. Maya Angelou's quote, "When you get, give. When you learn, teach" includes words I really appreciate. If you want to improve in your personal development and make progress in life, pay forward good deeds. **No matter what your age is, you can do something. You don't need any money; all you need is a big heart**. Give back to the next generation, be an example for the current generation, and help the experienced generation.

ACTION PLAN

Here are some "pay it forward" ideas:

✓ Write positive statements on 31 sticky notes and then place them in a colorful transparent jar. Before placing the lid on the jar, write on the top of lid: YOU ARE SPECIAL. Once complete, put the lid on the jar. Give this jar to an exceptional person in your life. Instruct them to remove a sticky note every day for positive encouragement. At the beginning of each month, give them 29–31 new sticky notes for their jar.

✓ Say "Hello," "Good morning," "Good day," or "Thank you," when appropriate, throughout the day.

✓ Offer to shovel (for free) an elderly couple's sidewalk or driveway after a snowstorm.

✓ Give someone a compliment.

✓ Volunteer.

✓ Smile at a kid.

✓ Leave a really good tip at a restaurant.

✓ When purchasing your coffee, buy a coffee for the person behind you in line.

✓ As you are walking by someone, tell them "You can do it," and keep walking. It will be a pleasant surprise, and I guarantee there will be something in their life they can relate this statement to.

Let's review some key points in part three:

- ✓ Surround yourself with OHP (Only Hungry People).
- ✓ Listening to your spirit can help you make progress in life. It is the common sense instinct that is guiding you in the right direction.
- ✓ Everyone who has done anything great has completed the accomplishment with fear.
- ✓ There are many actors, athletes, and everyday people who are always looking to not just reach their goals but crush them.
- ✓ Learning to appreciate your journey is progress. It builds your character.
- ✓ We have the power to make the world we envision but only if we have the courage to take the first step.
- ✓ Shifting our focus to family, curing deadly diseases, investing in education, and being great role models can be a start.
- ✓ Pain improves your character; it prepares you, increases you, and develops you.
- ✓ No matter what your age is, you can do something. You don't need any money; all you need is a big heart.

NOTES

What was reflective in this section that you will utilize immediately to help you make progress in your life?

Printed in the United States
By Bookmasters